SNAKES AND  REPTILES

by Brian Williams

Copyright © **ticktock Entertainment Ltd 2003**
First published in Great Britain in 2003 by ticktock Media Ltd.,
Unit 2, Orchard Business Centre, North Farm Road, Tunbridge Wells, Kent, TN2 3XF.

We would like to thank:
Lorna Cowan, Isolde McGeorge at Chester Zoo and Elizabeth Wiggans.
Illustrations by Simon Clare Creative Workshop.
Photography by Roddy Paine Photographic Studios: 4-5, 6-7, 8-9, 10-11, 12-13, 14-15,
16-17, 18-19, 20-21, 26-27.

Picture Credits:
Alamy images: 27tr. Corbis: 29tr. Natural Science Photos: 22-23,
24-25 (C.Dani – I.Jeske – Milano), 28-29 (Hal Beral).

ISBN 1 86007 349 2 pbk
ISBN 1 86007 339 5 hbk
Printed in Hong Kong

Contents

All words appearing in the text in bold, **like this**, are explained in the glossary.

Think...

What do snakes and other **reptiles** eat?

How do they catch their **prey**?

Are they friendly or dangerous to human beings?

Reptiles are cold-blooded animals with **scales**. Snakes, lizards, and turtles are all reptiles. There are more than 6,000 different kinds. **Prehistoric** dinosaurs were reptiles, too. But no reptiles today are as big as the giant dinosaurs!

Imagine...

If you were their prey, would you be able to escape from them?

It looks like you are about to find out...

Run!

Snakes cannot see very well.

They can track small animals by smell.

A hungry python grabs its prey with its teeth. Then it loops its body in coils around the animal.

It squeezes hard, **suffocating** the prey to dea

The python swallows its prey whole. This can take an hour, but one large meal lasts the python for weeks.

Yummy! Nice and full.

The python's mouth can open wide enough to swallow an animal bigger than its own head!

This is a ball python.

This African ball python is five feet long (about the height of a cow). This is short for a python. The longest ones can grow to 26 feet!

Don't squeeze me!

The ball python is named that because it rolls up in a ball when it is in danger.

Pythons do not have legs, but they do have tiny leg bones inside their bodies. This tells us their prehistoric relatives had legs.

This is a corn snake.

Corn snakes are also called **rat snakes**. They eat rats and mice that feed on crops, so farmers in the U.S. like having them around. Some people are scared of snakes, but this one cannot hurt people. It is not poisonous to human beings.

Snakes flick their tongues out to "taste" the air and see if they can sense an animal close by.

A snake has no eyelids.

Its eyes are always open—even when the snake is asleep.

Any food around here?

Snakes have Y-shaped tongues.

Snakes are not slimy to touch.

Their skin feels dry.

A corn snake lays its eggs in piles of rotting plants. This keeps the eggs warm. After a 60-day **incubation**, baby snakes wriggle out of the eggs and start hunting for food.

Some people keep corn snakes as pets.

Corn snakes can grow as long as five feet.

When a rattlesnake is threatened, it will lift the tip of its tail and rattle a warning. The rattle is made of hard scales.

The hard scales click together.

Rattle, rattle!

A rattlesnake kills with poison from its **fangs**. Snake poison is called **venom**.

When the rattlesnake shakes its tail, it makes a noise like a rattle.

The fangs are in here.

Rattlesnakes can weigh as much as a medium-sized dog (35 pounds)!

This is a rattlesnake.

Rattlesnakes live in hot **deserts** and hardly ever drink water. This diamondback rattlesnake can grow to over six feet long, as tall as a man.

Most females give birth to nine or ten live babies every two to three years.

Like all snakes, a rattlesnake outgrows its skin. It **sheds** its skin two or three times a year.

Time for a change.

The ground
is moving.

Whooahh!

Vipers are not big eaters. A Gaboon viper in a zoo once went for more than two years without eating!

The viper has the longest fangs of any venomous (poisonous) snake. The fangs fold back in the viper's top jaw. When the viper opens its mouth to bite, the fangs swing forward.

It is one of the most deadly poisonous snakes.

The fangs pump venom into the victim and can kill it in seconds!

Not too close!

It's a Gaboon viper.

The Gaboon viper's skin pattern helps the snake hide among the forest leaves. This is called **camouflage**. The Gaboon viper lives in Africa.

It is slow and usually stays out of sight. So luckily, the Gaboon viper hardly ever bites people!

Look at these nose horns and scaly lips.

Its fangs are about as long as your thumb!

Pit vipers have heat-sensitive pits, or indents, in their lips. The pits sense the viper's prey (small animals) in the dark.

What a
funny face!

Ha ha ha!

It's a cobra.

Cobras are the longest venomous snakes. The king cobra of Asia can grow to twelve feet long. Some cobras can spit venom at an enemy up to seven feet away. The poison blinds the enemy. This allows the snake to wriggle away to safety.

The venom comes from here!

The funny face is the back view of a cobra.
It has a hood of skin behind its head.
When it meets an enemy, the snake
rears up and spreads
its hood.

The hood makes the
cobra look bigger than
it really is. But if the
hood trick fails, the
cobra slithers away.

I'm big and mean!

These markings
help to camouflage
the snake among
the leaves
and twigs.

Cobras eat small animals,
birds, lizards, toads, and
even other snakes!

They can swivel each eye around.

Chameleons can see forward with one eye and backward with the other at the same time.

This is a chameleon.

Chameleons are lizards—reptiles with legs and tails. They move very slowly, lifting one foot at a time.

Its tongue is longer than its body!

To catch insects, spiders, and smaller lizards, the chameleon shoots out its tongue rapidly. On the tip of the tongue is a sticky spot that catches the prey.

It hangs onto a branch with its claws and curling tail.

Special skin **cells** allow the chameleon to change color.

Chameleons can change color. They can be green one minute and brown the next. This happens when the temperature or amount of light changes or if the chameleon senses danger.

Is this a rocky desert?

It eats the ants one at a time so eating dinner takes ages!

This lizard eats ants. It waits for a lin of ants to march past, then licks ther up with its tongue.

The lizard will eat 1,000 ants in a single meal!

Like cactus plants, these lizards are prickly all over.

Thorny devils grow to eight inches long, or the width of a school notebo

No! It's a thorny devil lizard.

Thorny devils live in Australia's hot **deserts**. Like all lizards, they spend their time in the sunshine. It takes them a while to warm up on cool mornings. If the midday sun gets too hot, they cool off under a shady rock.

thorns can help the lizard catch water.

I'm thirsty!

At night, dew forms on the lizard's back and trickles along the prickly path into its mouth. Then the lizard has a drink.

This is a bearded dragon.

This type of lizard lives in Australia. Lizards are always alert. They may look sleepy, basking in the sun, but in an instant they can scuttle away.

A frilly beard.

The lizard's beard is a frill of skin. The male can spread the frill to make itself look bigger and startle enemies.

It looks just like a mini-dinosaur!

All reptiles have scaly skin. The bearded dragon's feet are covered in scales, like the rest of its body.

Some lizards have no legs, so they look like snakes. But the bearded dragon has legs and feet with five toes on each foot.

Many bigger animals often eat lizards.

Each toe has a claw.

If a **predator** grabs the bearded dragon by its tail, the tail will break off. The lizard can escape. In time, a new tail will grow!

This is a hawksbill turtle.

Turtles are swimming reptiles. Hawksbill turtles live in the ocean in warm, **tropical** parts of the world.

Turtles are speedy swimmers.

They have shells just like tortoises.

A turtle uses its back flippers for steering.

Turtles most often swim in shallow water, where they can dive down to nibble sea sponges.

Female turtles crawl onto a beach, dig a hole, and lay their eggs in the sand. When the baby turtles hatch, they dash to the water.

The eggs have rubbery shells.

Many baby turtles are eaten by predators before they reach the safety of the sea.

To swim, turtles wave their front **flippers** up and down.

Sea turtles are **endangered**. People hunt them for their shells, and they get trapped in fishing nets. Turtles lay their eggs on beaches, where they are easily disturbed.

GLOSSARY

CAMOUFLAGE Colors or markings that match an animal's surrounding and help keep it hidden.

CELLS Tiny parts of an animal's body. People, animals, and plants are all made of cells.

DESERTS Hot, dry places where very few people, animals, or plants live.

ENDANGERED When there are not many of a kind of animal left, and the remaining animals are in danger of being hunted by human beings or of losing their habitat (the place where they live).

FANGS Snake fangs are special teeth that inject venom into the snake's victim.

FLIPPERS Legs that have become flattened, like paddles, for swimming.

INCUBATION The time that an egg spends in a warm place, while the animal inside grows and gets ready to hatch.

PREDATOR An animal that lives by hunting, killing, and eating other animals.

PREHISTORIC Belonging to a time millions of years before people lived on earth.

PREY An animal that is hunted for food by another animal.

REPTILES Animals that include snakes, turtles, lizards, crocodiles, and alligators. They are cold-blooded, have scaly skins and live in warm places.

SCALES Tough, flat sections of skin that protect the bodies of reptiles and fish.

SHED To cast off, or drop, skin or hair.

SUFFOCATING To choke or stop something from breathing.

TROPICAL Places where it is hot and very rainy.

VENOM Poison made in special glands (parts of the body) in some snakes.

INDEX